LA CIUDAD EN TI
THE CITY WITHIN YOU

LA CIUDAD EN TI
THE CITY WITHIN YOU
© Karla Marrufo / Allison A. deFreese / Monika Malgorzata Gabrys /Cathexis Northwest Press

No part of this book may be reproduced without written permission of the
publisher or author, except in reviews and articles.

First Printing: 2023

ISBN: 978-1-952869-85-3

Cover image by Monika Malgorzata Gabrys
Editing & Design by C. M. Tollefson
Cathexis Northwest Press

cathexisnorthwestpress.com

LA CIUDAD EN TI
THE CITY WITHIN YOU
BY KARLA MARRUFO
TRANSLATED FROM THE SPANISH BY ALLISON A. DEFREESE

Cathexis Northwest Press

**OBRA GANADORA DEL
XVI PREMIO DE POESÍA "JOSÉ DÍAZ
BOLIO" CENTRO CULTURAL PROHISPEN,
MÉXICO**

**WINNER OF THE XVI "JOSÉ DÍAZ BOLIO" PRIZE IN POETRY
(XVI PREMIO DE POESÍA "JOSÉ DÍAZ BOLIO"),
CENTRO CULTURAL PROHISPEN, MEXICO**

Translator's Note

As novelist Anita Desai suggests, "wherever you go becomes a part of you somehow." Karla Marrufo understands that what you've left also remains within you. These are not cities in architecture only, they are emotional landscapes, and in them the feeling of being "foreign" or "other" lingers whether the narrator is home or abroad. There are hints (that I've faithfully translated, though not explained) that "the city within you" might be in the Yucatán; one of the "yellow cities in our dreams," a place where it is customary to eat twelve "lucky grapes" (one for each month) to welcome the New Year and people are "untouched by [...] winter in a warm place." Yet both origin and destination could be anywhere we have lived or arrived at "light as certain birds" with the toes of our sneakers scuffed. From traveler to refugee, *The City Within You* speaks to the heart of human movement, to being welcomed—or unwelcome to the point of persecution (and worse)—to fleeing from or fleeing to the familiar, the unknown.

TABLA DE CONTENIDO

Otras ciudades	4
Cualquier Ícaro	6
Mudanza	8
#SiMeMatan	12
Año nuevo	16
Los puentes verdaderos	20

TABLE OF CONTENTS

Other Cities	5
Any Icarus	7
The Move	9
#IfTheyKillMe	13
The New Year	17
The True Bridges	21

*La ciudad irá en ti siempre. Volverás
a las mismas calles. Y en los mismos
suburbios llegará tu vejez;
en la misma casa amanecerás.
Pues la ciudad es siempre la misma. Otra
no busques –no la hay–
ni caminos ni barco para ti.
La vida que aquí perdiste
la has destruido en toda la tierra.*

Kavafis

This city will always pursue you.

You'll walk the same streets, grow old

in the same neighborhoods, turn grey in these same houses [...]

Now that you've wasted your life here, in this small corner,

you've destroyed it everywhere in the world.

Cavafy

OTRAS CIUDADES

a través de los mares

a pesar de los tiempos

sólo quería confirmar que existes,

que te encuentras intacta en la nota más sencilla

de un invierno sin frío

quería decir que en el sueño hay ciudades amarillas

hechas de otras ciudades

y que quizá en alguna te encontré

mirando tu reflejo en un ojo de agua

sólo quería dejar constancia del crujir del viento

sin hablar de desmesuras ni desastres naturales

para poder olvidar ese temblor seco que nos amarra la sonrisa

cuando nos advertimos solos

y sin nombres propios

sólo quise guardar tus huellas

en un secreto rincón de mis manos

    por si acaso

    algún día

    aventuro el camino de regreso.

OTHER CITIES

across the seas

and despite the times

i only wanted to know you exist still

untouched by those faint signs

of winter in a warm place

i wanted to tell you—there are yellow cities in our dreams,

cities built from other cities,

and perhaps i found you

in one of them:

gazing at your own reflection

in the water from a spring

i only wanted to leave a record of the rustling wind,

without mentioning excess or natural disasters,

to forget this dry tremor

that binds our smiles

when we notice we are alone,

and without names of our own

i only wanted to keep your traces

in a secret corner of my hand

    in case

    someday

    i venture back that way.

CUALQUIER ÍCARO

nunca supe su nombre

pero vi su muerte en el instante más claro

escuché su cuerpo

y su agrietarse,

sus huesos al final de la agonía,

su sangre despierta

ampliándose con una espesura

que sonaba a fruta llena de tiempo.

tampoco supe su mirada;

pues cuando llegué a ella

sólo encontré una neblina profunda,

que hasta entonces desconocía.

no supe el ritmo de sus pisadas

ni la aspereza de su lengua

ni el crujir del aire en su ladrido

sólo supe de la precisión de la muerte

y del mal augurio

implícito

en el vuelo de cualquier Ícaro.

ANY ICARUS

i never knew her name

but i watched her die in the clearest instant

heard her body

open, the crack of bones

at the end of her agony,

her blood awake and spreading

with the thickness of fruit ripe with time.

nor did i know her gaze;

for when i arrived at her side

a heavy mist i had never known

until that moment was all that remained.

i never knew the rhythm of her footsteps

the roughness of her tongue

the snap of air when she barked

i only knew death's precision at the end

and the bad omen

implicit

in the flight of any Icarus.

MUDANZA

llegamos al mediodía

    maletas en mano

el sol era un cuadro de cemento

recostado a nuestros pies,
el cielo un golpe seco,

un mordisco de polvo,

un raspón en las mejillas

sílaba por sílaba se fueron abriendo las palabras francas:

    alcantarilla   cisterna   vecindario   extranjero   dormitorio

        bienvenida

sílaba por sílaba las revelaciones más mudas:

    de la mano de alguien uno aprende a respirar el aire

        que es humo

    a saborear los amaneceres de una ciudad desconocida

    a reencontrarse en sueños

    a prometerse no vivir nunca de prestado

    de la mano de alguien el mundo se hace a veces uno, suficiente,

        comprensible como un juego de niños

        mientras dure

    de la mano de alguien la noche disuelve sus fantasmas dejándonos el ropaje de una

        historia inconclusa

    de la mano de alguien,

THE MOVE

we arrived at midday,

    with our luggage in hand

the sun a cement square

stretching out beneath our feet,

the sky a sharp blow to the face—

a sting of dust,

a scratch on the cheek

syllable by syllable, the valve of honest words

slowly opened:

    sewer   cistern   foreigner   neighborhood   bedroom

                                      welcome

syllable by syllable, this drip of silent revelations:

    hand in hand, we learn to breathe the air,

        inhaling only smoke

      to savor the sunrise of an unknown city,

      to discover it again in dreams,

      to promise we will never live on loans

    hand in hand, sometimes the world is made whole, and that is enough,

      easy as child's play

      while it lasts

    hand in hand, the night dissolves with its ghosts, leaving us only the cloak

      of an unfinished story

    together,

con la presión de su sangre corriendo al mismo compás de nuestro

  miedo, uno aprende a recordar

                   por obligación

                   por ternura

                   por rabia

                   por vocación

                   porque no hay más

llegamos al mediodía

    ligeros como ciertas aves

la punta de mis tenis roídos había perdido la brújula,

el olfato,

pero se aventuró un poco hacia la sangre,

hacia el ahora río rojo inaugurando un cauce

hacia la boca del alcantarillado

sílaba por sílaba corrieron las explicaciones:

    la altura del edificio   el vértigo   el peligro

mi mano quedó sola,

        desde entonces   para siempre

cerrándose sobre sí para mirar la vida

cuando se transforma

en materia oscura.

                    blood pulsing to the heartbeats

                    of our fear, we learn to remember

                                out of obligation

                                out of fondness

                                out of rage

                                or by vocation

                                because this is all there is

we arrived at midday

    light as certain birds

the toes of my scuffed sneakers had lost their direction

their sense of smell,

but ventured forward a little anyway

toward blood,

toward the river, now red, unveiling a channel

that leads to the mouth of the sewer

syllable by syllable the excuses flowed:

    the height of the building   vertigo   dangerous

    since then and   forever

my hand remains alone,

closes in on itself and watches as life

transforms

into dark matter.

#SIMEMATAN

dirán que era antisocial, depresiva, arrogante

que siempre tuvo la frente muy alta,

la lengua muy larga

y la falda muy corta

que mantuvo en la friendzone a varios hombres buenos

y que sin embargo solía usar vestidos escotados y cortísimos

dirán que viajaba sola o sólo con amigas que es lo mismo

dirán que vivía sola

caminaba sola

hacía las compras sola

paseaba al perro sola

se paseaba a sí misma sola

que se dormía en trenes, aviones, autobuses,

como esperando a que algo sucediera

dirán que nunca se casó ni tuvo hijos,

que despreció desde siempre su instinto maternal

dirán que era atea, agnóstica, esotérica y coqueteaba con la santería

que el orden impecable en su casa delataba sin duda un trastorno psiquiátrico

dirán que a veces se desaparecía semanas enteras

#IFTHEYKILLME

they will say she was antisocial, depressed, arrogant

that she always held her head high

had a big mouth

wore short skirts

that she kept several good men in her *friendzone*

yet always wore low-cut dresses that were far too short

they will say she traveled alone—or with other women, which is the same thing

that she lived alone

walked alone

shopped alone

walked the dog alone

went out by herself—alone

that she fell asleep on trains, planes, busses—

as if waiting for something to happen

they will say she never married or had children

that she loathed maternal instinct

that she was atheist, agnostic, esoteric, dabbled in santaria

that the immaculate neatness of her home was undeniable evidence of mental illness

that she never really had any friends

dirán que sin embargo se le solía ver acompañada de

lesbianas, homosexuales, transgénero, teatreros,

músicos, literatos en general y poetas en particular, todos ellos tatuados, con

los cabellos de colores y perforados de las narices y otras partes menos

decentes

dirán que a veces se desaparecía semanas enteras

    seguramente para dedicarse a los

    sacrificios que exige la santería

    seguramente para participar

    de orgías pérfidas con esa caterva de hippiosos

    seguramente para empastillarse hasta

    la inconsciencia

y luego reaparecía como si todo estuviera tan normal

dirán que bebía demasiado

dirán que era abstemia y eso no es normal

dirán que parecía que siempre estaba mariguana

dirán que nunca fumó pero seguro se metía otras cosas

dirán que la mataron porque para un ser así no había lugar.

they will, however, say she was frequently seen in the company of:
gays, lesbians, transgendered women and men, people from the theater, musicians, writers in general and poets in particular—all of them tattooed, with hair dyed the colors of the rainbow, their noses pierced—as well as their unmentionables

they will say she sometimes disappeared for a whole week
    that she must have performed the rituals
    and sacrifices that santeria demands
    that she must have joined that pack of
    hippies in depraved orgies

    that she must have popped pills until falling
    unconscious
only to reappear as if everything was normal

they will say she drank too much
they will say she never drank, and that was strange
they will say she always seemed baked
they will say she never smoked but must have done other things

they will say they killed her because there was no place for a creature like her in this world.

AÑO NUEVO

y en todas partes llega la consigna del tiempo

:

celebrar cada ciclo como si fuera irrepetible

así llegaron los primeros zumbidos de la noche
anunciando que algo se escapaba hacia los cielos
algo más que la luz
      lo fugaz tal vez
      lo más oscuro que cada uno oculta en la paz de sus secretos
por eso el fuego es de artificio, ahora lo sé.

decían que las calles se vestían de alegría
pero yo sólo advertía su desnudez
la mano invisible que soltaba la coleta de la dicha

había despertado en un lugar extraño
con la tristeza grave de quien nada entiende sobre uvas
ni deseos
y así seguí por la tarde

THE NEW YEAR

and so tonight time's cry arrives everywhere

:

celebrate each cycle as if it were one-in-a-lifetime

and so the first buzzings
of night coming to life
announcing something
besides light
escaping upward toward the sky

something fleeting, perhaps
the darkest things we each hide in the peace of our secrets
that's why fireworks aren't fire, i see this now.

the streets were decked in joy (or so they told me)
but i only noticed their nakedness

the invisible hand that unbinds the ponytail
of good fortune

in this strange place i awoke
with deepest sorrow like one who knows nothing of grapes
or of wish-making.
nothing changed that afternoon

paseando mi tristeza en bicicleta

sorteando los agujeros del asfalto

y el rumor de un racimo de borrachos

amándose hasta las entrañas,

aullándose lealtad frente a la luna.

sonreímos por fin

de candidez y de nostalgia

por aquellas cosas que creímos nuestras

por nuestras manos inútiles

por la pasión con que algún día

nos aferramos a otro suelo.

regresamos a la casa nueva

vacías   profundamente vacías

mi tristeza, mi bicicleta roja
y yo

así sin nada   así libres

dejando todo el tiempo y el espacio

limpios

para el ciclo que habría de iniciar en unas horas.

i spent it on my bike

taking my sadness for a ride dodging

potholes in the pavement

and the muttering clusters of drunks

utterly in love with themselves,

howling their devotion under the moon.

finally we smiled

out of naivety and nostalgia

at the things we believed ours

at our useless hands

at the urgency with which we will someday

cast anchor on other lands.

my sadness, my red bike

and i

returned to our new home

empty   completely depleted—

with nothing   free

leaving time and space

clean

for the cycle that must commence again

just a few hours hence.

LOS PUENTES VERDADEROS

pero a veces digo "la ciudad despierta"
y los pájaros la nombran con su trinar alargado
        con los hilos de un eco intraducible
              verde
que se expande como onda en aguas quietas

hay algo en el azul amanecer que puede ser revelación o espejismo
        suspenso pasadizo de quietud
          hacia el alabeo de las cosas cuando se saben vivas

la ciudad se levanta para sí
pero abre al alba ciertos ríos que no existen
el temblor de unas montañas que no llegan
        pero hacia estas costas miran

son sitios invisibles:
        recintos de los ecos de las aves
        sin forma ya
        sin signo alguno

THE TRUE BRIDGES

but sometimes i say *the city*

is waking as the birds name it

with their prolonged song—

    the threads of

                    green

echoes that have no translation,

spread like waves on quiet waters

something of a revelation or mirage

comes with the blue dawn,

    with the suspense of this passage from calmness

    into motion, just as objects curve

    when they know they are alive.

the city awakens by itself,

though dawn opens certain rivers that don't exist,

making way for the trembling mountains

that have yet to arrive,

    but are already looking toward these coasts

invisible places:

    spaces that echo with birds

    formless,

    without any sign whatsoever

digo la ciudad despierta y yo con ella

    aunque detrás de mí se erijan

        sueño adentro en la sangre

los puentes verdaderos.

    i say *the city is waking*, and i awaken with it
        though behind me they keep building
            the dreams that flow inside my veins
the true bridges.

Translator and poet are grateful to the following publications in which the English translations of poems from this chapbook first appeared, including:

Apofenie ("Any Icarus");

Eunoia Review ("#IfTheyKillMe" and "The New Year");

Los Angeles Review Online ("Other Cities" and "The True Bridges");

YourImpossibleVoice ("The Move")

The English-language excerpt from Kavafis' longer poem is the version from Princeton University Press (1975), translated by Edmund Keeley and Philip Sherrard.

Poet's bio: Karla Marrufo is author of eight books including novels, poetry collections, chapbooks, plays, and works of literary criticism. Her work has won prestigious awards including: Mexico's National Wilberto Cantón Award in Playwriting, the XVI José Díaz Bolio Poetry Prize, and the National Dolores Castro Prize for Women. She also received a fellowship from the Programa de Estímulo a la Creación y al Desarrollo Artístico en Yucatán (the PECDA, or Program for the Expansion and Development of Creativity and the Arts in the Yucatán), which resulted in the publication of her book *Mérida lo invisible / Mérida the Invisible* (Consejo Editorial de la Secretaría de la Cultura y las Artes de Yucatán). Her recent books of verse include *La Dulzura de los naufragios / The Sweetness of Shipwrecks* (2020) and *Si Mérida tuviera puentes / If Mérida Had Bridges* (2021).

Translator's bio: Allison A. deFreese is a poet and literary translator whose books of verse include *Nurdles and Other Poems* (2022) and *The Night with James Dean and Other Prose Poems* (winner of Cathexis Northwest Press' 2022 chapbook competition). Her translations of Karla Marrufo's work also appear in *Another Chicago Magazine*, *New England Review*, *SAND Journal Berlin's* 10th Anniversary Issue, and other publications. She translated Marrufo's novel *Flame Trees in May* (Dalkey Archive Press and Deep Vellum Publishing, May, 2023).

Also Available from Cathexis Northwest Press:

Something To Cry About
by Robert Krantz

Suburban Hermeneutics
by Ian Cappelli

God's Love Is Very Busy
by David Seung

that one time we were almost people
by Christian Czaniecki

Fever Dream/Take Heart
by Valyntina Grenier

The Book of Night & Waking
by Clif Mason

Dead Birds of New Zealand
by Christian Czaniecki

The Weathering of Igneous Rockforms in High-Altitude Riparian Environments
by John Belk

If A Fish
by George Burns

How to Draw a Blank
by Collin Van Son

En Route
by Jesse Wolfe

sky bright psalms
by Temple Cone

Moonbird
by Henry G. Stanton

southern athiest. oh, honey
by d. e. fulford

Bruises, Birthmarks & Other Calamities
by Nadine Klassen

Wanted: Comedy, Addicts
by AR Dugan

They Curve Like Snakes
by David Alexander McFarland

the catalog of daily fears
by Beth Dufford

Shops Close Too Early
by Josh Feit

<u>Vanity Unfair and Other Poems</u>
by Robert Eugene Rubino

<u>Destructive Heresies</u>
by Milo E. Gorgevska

<u>Bodies of Separation</u>
by Chim Sher Ting

<u>The Night with James Dean and Other Prose Poems</u>
by Allison A. deFreese

<u>About Time</u>
by Julie Benesh

<u>Suspended</u>
by Ellen White Rook

<u>The Unempty Spaces Between</u>
by Louis Efron

<u>Quomodo probatur in conflatorio</u>
by Nick Roberts

<u>Suspended</u>
by Ellen White Rook

<u>Call Me Not Ishmael but the Sea</u>
by J. Martin Daughtry

<u>Wild Evolution</u>
by Naomi Leimsider

<u>Coming To Terms</u>
by Peter Sagnella

<u>Acta</u>
by Patrick Wilcox

<u>Honeymoon Shoes</u>
by Valyntina Grenier

<u>Practising Ascending</u>
by Nadine Hitchiner

<u>Home Visit</u>
by Michal Rubin

Cathexis Northwest Press

www.ingramcontent.com/pod-product-compliance
Lightning Source LLC
Chambersburg PA
CBHW030141100526
44592CB00011B/989